Food Intruders

INVISIBLE CREATURES LURKING IN YOUR FOOD

by Karen M. Leet

CONSULTANT:
DEBORAH PHILLIPS, DOCTOR OF EDUCATION
LECTURER, DEPARTMENT OF MICROBIOLOGY
MIAMI UNIVERSITY, OXFORD, OHIO

CAPSTONE PRESS
a capstone imprint

Edge Books are published by Capstone Press,
151 Good Counsel Drive, P.O. Box 669, Mankato, Minnesota 56002.
www.capstonepub.com

Copyright © 2012 by Capstone Press, a Capstone imprint.
All rights reserved.
No part of this publication may be reproduced in whole or in part,
or stored in a retrieval system, or transmitted in any form or by any means,
electronic, mechanical, photocopying, recording, or otherwise, without
written permission of the publisher.
For information regarding permission, write to Capstone Press,
151 Good Counsel Drive, P.O. Box 669, Dept. R, Mankato, Minnesota 56002.

 Books published by Capstone Press are manufactured with paper containing at least 10 percent post-consumer waste.

Library of Congress Cataloging-in-Publication Data
Leet, Karen M.
  Food intruders : invisible creatures lurking in your food / Leet, Karen.
    p. cm.—(Edge books. Tiny creepy creatures.)
  Summary: "Describes both harmful and harmless microbes that may be found in foods"—Provided by publisher.
  Includes bibliographical references and index.
  ISBN 978-1-4296-6532-2 (library binding)
  ISBN 978-1-4296-7273-3 (paperback)
  1. Bacteria--Juvenile literature. I. Title. II. Series.

QR57.L44 2012
616.9'201—dc22   2011001979

Editorial Credits
Kristen Mohn, editor; Veronica Correia, designer; Svetlana Zhurkin,
   media researcher; Eric Manske, production specialist

Photo Credits
Alamy: Michael Gilday, 28 (bottom), Nigel Cattlin, 15, North Wind Picture Archives, 9; CDC: Janice Haney Carr, 16, 21 (top); Dreamstime: Uwe Malitz, 13 (bottom); iStockphoto: Brian Maudsley, cover (bottom), Lew Zimmerman, 7 (bottom), sumnersgraphicsinc, 17; Library of Congress, 11; Shutterstock/ampFotoStudio, 28 (top), buruhtan, cover (top), 1, Christopher Meade, 8 (bottom), dragon_fang, 12 (left), Eduard Kyslynskyy, 18 (bottom), Elena Elisseeva, 5 (back), 14 (left), Eric Isselée, 19, Grauvision, 27 (bottom), Joerg Beuge, 5 (bottom), jon le-bon, 26, Julija Sapic, 10, Kheng Guan Toh, 25, Monkey Business Images, 23, naluwan, 29, Nicolas McComber, 18 (top), Oleksiy Fedorov, back cover and background throughout, ra3rn, 8 (top), Robert Crow, 20–21, Sergey Peterman, 12 (right), sil63, 14 (right), visi.stock, 22, Yai, 28 (middle), zcw, 13 (top); Svetlana Zhurkin, 27 (back); Visuals Unlimited/Dennis Kunkel Microscopy, 7 (back)

Printed in the United States of America in Stevens Point, Wisconsin.
032011   006111WZF11

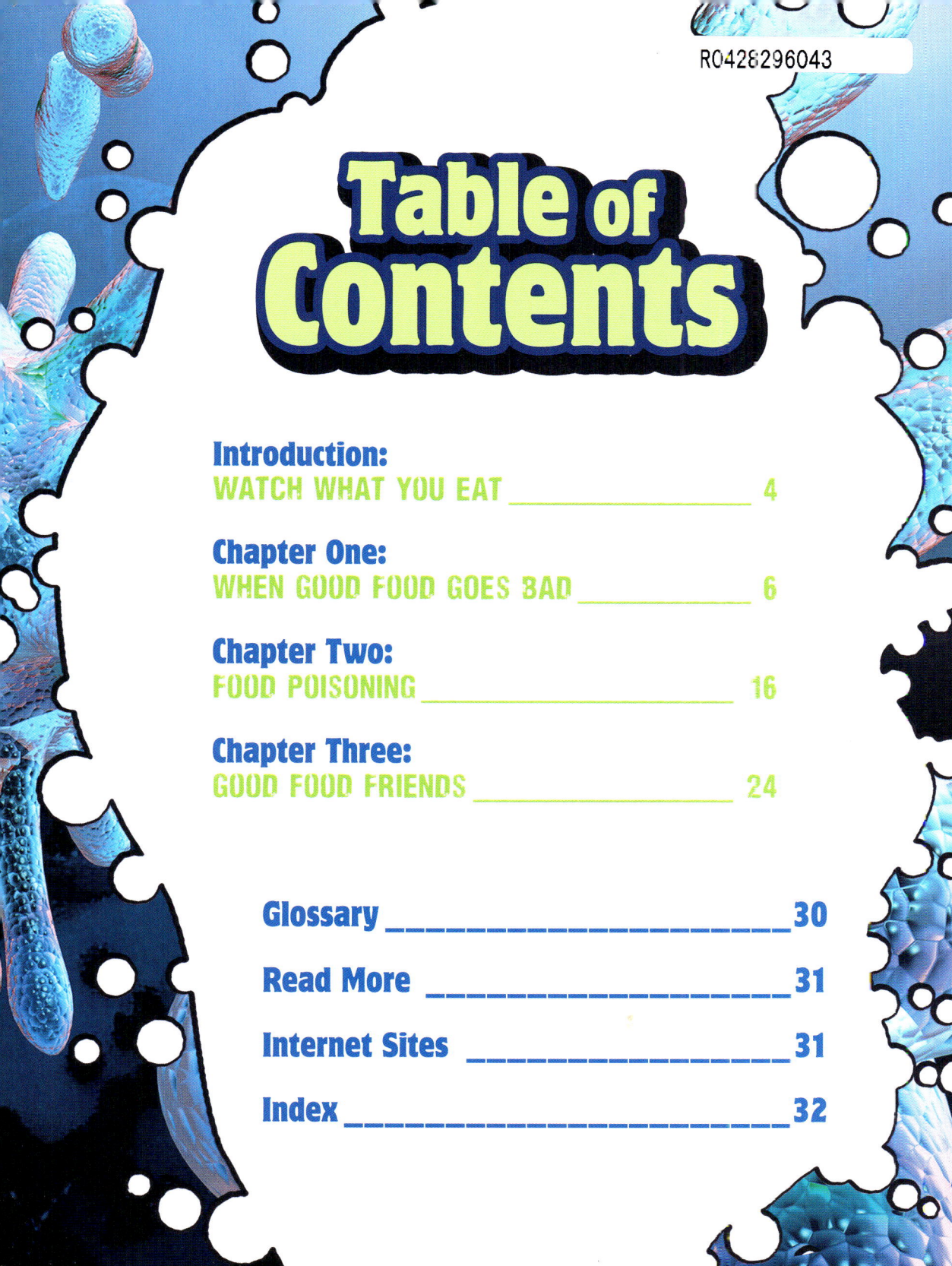

Table of Contents

Introduction:
WATCH WHAT YOU EAT 4

Chapter One:
WHEN GOOD FOOD GOES BAD 6

Chapter Two:
FOOD POISONING 16

Chapter Three:
GOOD FOOD FRIENDS 24

Glossary 30

Read More 31

Internet Sites 31

Index 32

Introduction

WATCH WHAT YOU EAT

Hungry? Before you bite into that apple, think about it. Was it washed? And is that milk still fresh? If not, you may be about to eat a mouthful of multiplying **microbes**.

We eat plenty of microbes every day without realizing it. These tiny living things are on every surface, including our food.

All microbes keep very busy. Microbe action creates good things like cheese and chocolate. Microbes can also cause bad things like vomiting and diarrhea.

Like it or not, they're here to stay. So you may as well get to know these food friends and foes.

microbe—a living thing that is too small to see without a microscope

Chapter 1
WHEN GOOD FOOD GOES BAD

Something's growing on the leftover spaghetti at the back of the fridge. Yuck. It's mold, a kind of **fungus**. Mold likes warm, wet places best, but it can still grow on refrigerated foods. That's its mission—to grow and spread, gobbling any natural matter in its path.

Microscopic bits called spores spread the mold. They drift in the air like dust specks and land on food. No place is totally safe. Whether food is on the counter or in the fridge, sooner or later mold spores find it. When enough spores gather and reproduce, you can see them decorating your food like fuzzy frosting. Gross!

fungus—a living thing that breaks down natural material
microscopic—too small to be seen without a microscope

mold spores

What you can't see are the threadlike branches that grow deep into the food. Mold reaches farther into your food than just the fuzzy part you see on top. That fuzzy stuff is the spores, which are held up by tiny stalks. Peek through a microscope and you'll see that mold looks like tiny mushrooms.

moldy salsa

Ewww Fact!
Microbes grow fastest between 40 and 140 degrees Fahrenheit (4 and 60 degrees Celsius). Some microbes can still grow inside the fridge or freezer, but not as fast.

WHAT'S ON YOUR SANDWICH?

Bread is a common target for mold. Spores can spread from the air onto the bread when you open the bread sack. Or a few spores might already be in the package. It can get warm and moist inside a bread bag—perfect for mold growth. Soon, you have fuzzy, colorful bread.

One fungus, called black bread mold, makes a dark fuzz on bread. You might also find a fuzzy, blue-green surprise spreading on your bread. It's *Penicillium*, and it often grows on cheese and other foods too. The cool thing about this mold is that the medicine penicillin is made from it. That's an **antibiotic** that helps fight infections.

Penicillium

antibiotic—a drug that kills bacteria and is used to cure infections

Witchcraft or Bad Bread?

In 1692 in Salem, Massachusetts, several young girls got sick. They twitched, moaned, and felt like someone was poking them with pins. A doctor said the girls must be under a witch's spell. Soon, many women, and some men, were accused of being witches and were put to death.

Two hundred years later, a researcher suggested a fungus might have been to blame. This fungus grows on grain. People who eat bread made from infected grain get sick like the girls in Salem did. Perhaps the Salem witch scare was caused by bad bread, not witches.

Salem witch trials

RED BREAD

Possibly the weirdest bread spoiler is not a fungus but a **bacterium** that's only one one-thousandth of a millimeter long. It causes wet red spots on bread and has the disgusting name of bleeding bread.

Health experts say not to eat moldy food—or "bleeding" food either. Molds can cause breathing and allergy problems. Some molds make a poison called mycotoxin, which can make people very sick. If you find moldy or rotting food, throw it away and clean up the area where you found it. You don't want any of those microbes spreading around.

bacterium—a single-celled microscopic creature that exists everywhere in nature

STINKY DRINK

What stinks in the fridge? It's rotten milk. Bacteria gone wild is what you smell. Milk, and most foods like fruits, veggies, and raw meat, already have bacteria in them. But the food only smells bad when too many bacteria have grown.

Louis Pasteur

A long time ago, milk used to have many more microbes in it. Some were very dangerous, such as the bacteria that cause tuberculosis, a deadly disease. That was before French scientist Louis Pasteur discovered a way to kill the harmful bacteria. In the 1860s, he found that heating milk to 160°F (71°C) would help keep it safe. This process is called **pasteurization**. Now milk and some other liquids like juice are pasteurized to get rid of most harmful microbes.

pasteurization—heating process for killing harmful microbes in milk and some other liquids

TOUGH MICROBES

But some bacteria aren't killed by pasteurization. These few tough microbes start to grow even in the fridge. Cold temps slow their growth, but at the milk expiration date these microbes build up. By a few days past that date, they're spoiling the milk and causing it to stink.

Several kinds of bacteria start making changes in the milk. One of these is a rod-shaped bacteria called *Lactobacillus*. It turns the milk sugar, or lactose, into a sour substance called lactic acid. Once that happens, not even sugary cereal will make this milk taste good again.

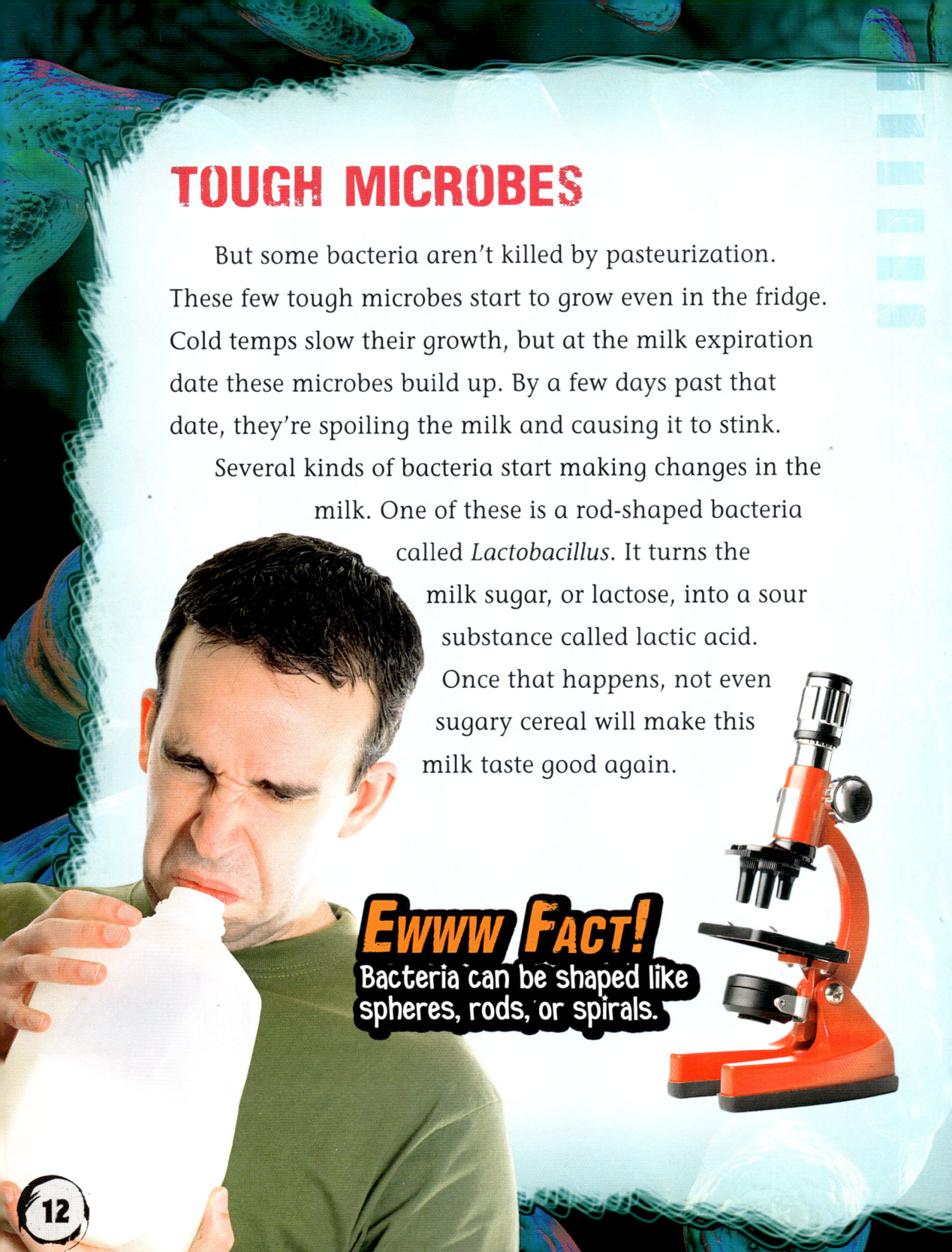

Ewww Fact!
Bacteria can be shaped like spheres, rods, or spirals.

SQUISHY FRUIT AND VEGGIES

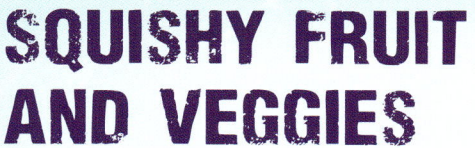

Black bananas and mushy apples are a sign that you have fungus in your fruit bowl. After all, molds have to eat, too, don't they? Actually, they don't eat. They just absorb their food. Mold latches on to a food supply, breaks it down, and takes in the **nutrients**.

But after that food is absorbed, it has to go somewhere. Exit waste! Mold produces waste products that look and smell bad. These waste products cause food to rot. They also create the unpleasant smell coming at you.

nutrient—a substance needed by a living thing to stay healthy

HUNGRY FUNGI

There is a long list of fungi that can damage or destroy your afternoon snack. One of the nasty intruders is gray mold rot, which makes gray fuzz on fruit surfaces. Crown rot is a fungus that blackens bananas. And soft rot fungus loves everything from cantaloupe to cucumbers to carrots. So eat your fresh fruits and veggies—before the hungry fungi do.

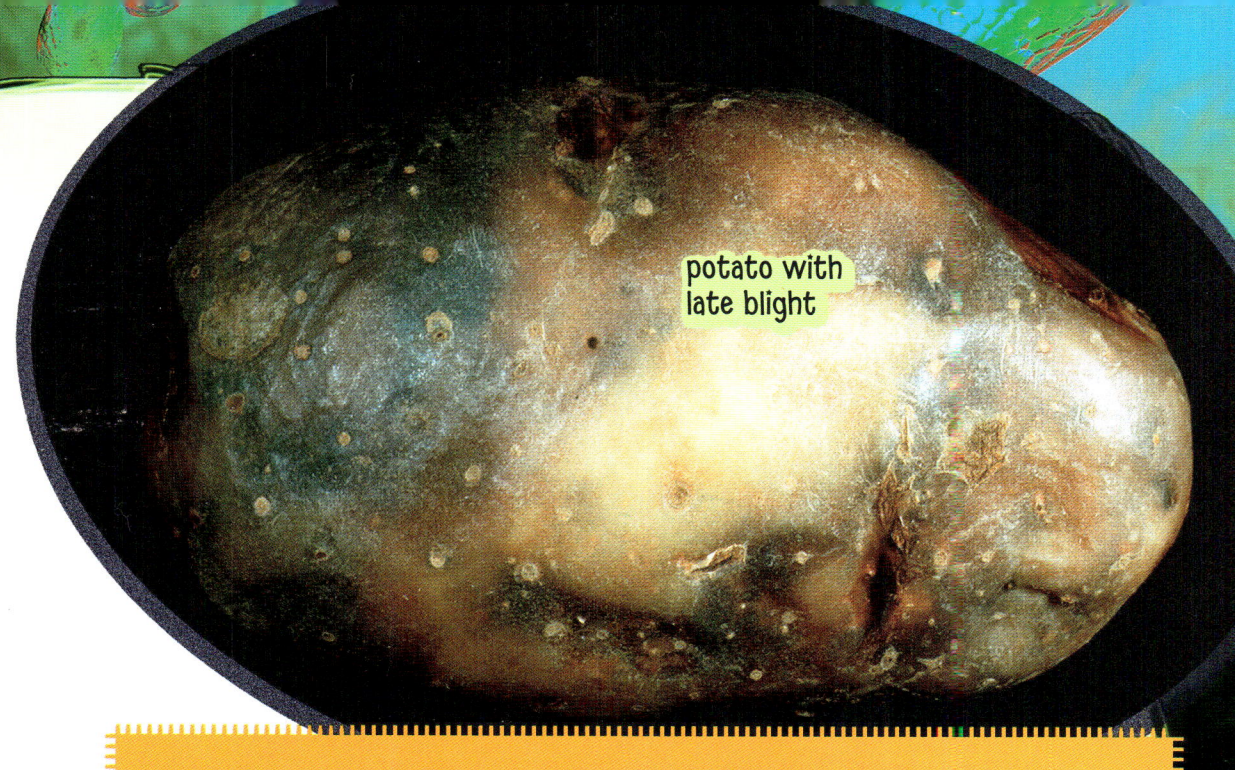

potato with late blight

Something Rotten in Ireland

In the mid-1800s, potatoes rotted in the fields across Ireland. The potatoes were black and squishy and gave off a horrible smell. For many Irish people, potatoes were the main food supply. Without potatoes, up to 1 million people starved. More than 1 million others left Ireland to find work and food. Many rushed to America.

It was the Irish Potato Famine, caused by a fungus known as late blight. Cool, moist weather in Ireland was perfect for fungus, but it was terrible for potatoes.

Chapter 2
FOOD POISONING

Your best friend gobbled a half-cooked burger yesterday. Today he's stuck in the bathroom with diarrhea. What happened? *Salmonella* happened. These one-celled, rod-shaped bacteria cause more than 1 million cases of illness in the United States each year.

There are more than 2,300 types of *Salmonella,* and about 200 of those can cause human illness. One type, called *Salmonella* Enteritidis, is the most common cause of food poisoning. It causes harm by absorbing nutrients and competing with helpful microbes in your body.

Salmonella

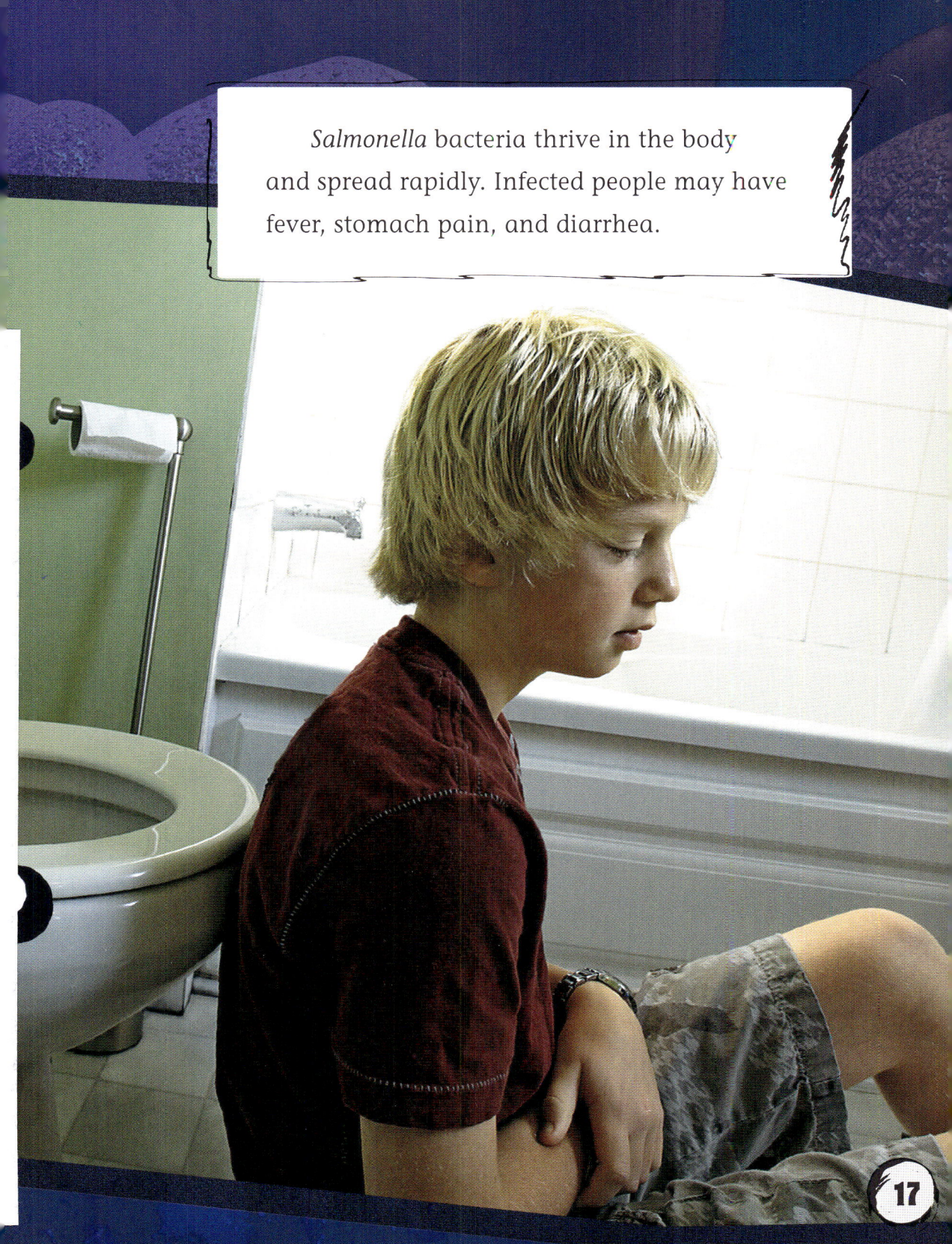

Salmonella bacteria thrive in the body and spread rapidly. Infected people may have fever, stomach pain, and diarrhea.

INVISIBLE DANGER

Salmonella can be found in raw or undercooked food, especially in meat, chicken, and eggs. You can't see, smell, or taste this bacteria on your food. But if you eat it, you may get sick. Infected people can also spread these dangerous germs. This is especially true if they don't wash their hands carefully after using the bathroom.

One of the worst *Salmonella* **outbreaks** in the United States came from an unexpected source—ice cream. In 1994 more than 200,000 people got very sick. It turned out an ingredient for the ice cream was carried in tanker trucks. The trucks were **contaminated** with *Salmonella* from egg products in an earlier load. The trucks weren't cleaned well enough to kill the harmful bacteria.

outbreak—when a number of people get sick at the same time from the same germ source
contaminated—unfit for use because of contact with a harmful substance

Ewww Fact!

Salmonella is often found on reptiles, such as turtles. It doesn't usually make the animal sick, but it can definitely make you sick. Always wash your hands well after touching a reptile.

A Dangerous Cook

In New York in the early 1900s, there were some mysterious outbreaks of typhoid fever. This serious disease is caused by a kind of *Salmonella* bacterium. Infected people suffered from fevers, headaches, sore throats, and stomach pain. There was no cure, and some people died. Health officials hunted for the cause of the outbreaks.

Soon they suspected a cook named Mary Mallon. They thought the food she prepared was making people sick. They tracked her down, tested her, and found she carried typhoid germs. These germs are passed in poop and pee. If infected people don't wash their hands carefully, typhoid can spread to others. Mary Mallon was locked up in a hospital to keep her from spreading germs. She became known as "Typhoid Mary."

MICROBES THAT MAKE THE NEWS

Escherichia coli is another bad bacteria when it's found on your food. Outbreaks of sickness from *E. coli* make headlines. Hundreds of people can be affected. One dangerous type of *E. coli*, 0157:H7, causes diarrhea, vomiting, and weakness. In severe cases, problems like blood infections or kidney failure may kill the infected person.

Like *Salmonella*, *E. coli* bacteria live in animal intestines. *E. coli* is commonly found in raw or undercooked beef. The illness it causes is sometimes called the hamburger disease. Health experts recommend you always order your burgers "well done" to avoid it.

Ewww Fact!
Reusable grocery bags are a great idea, but they bring home more than food. They can carry microbes such as *E. coli*, so wash them before reusing.

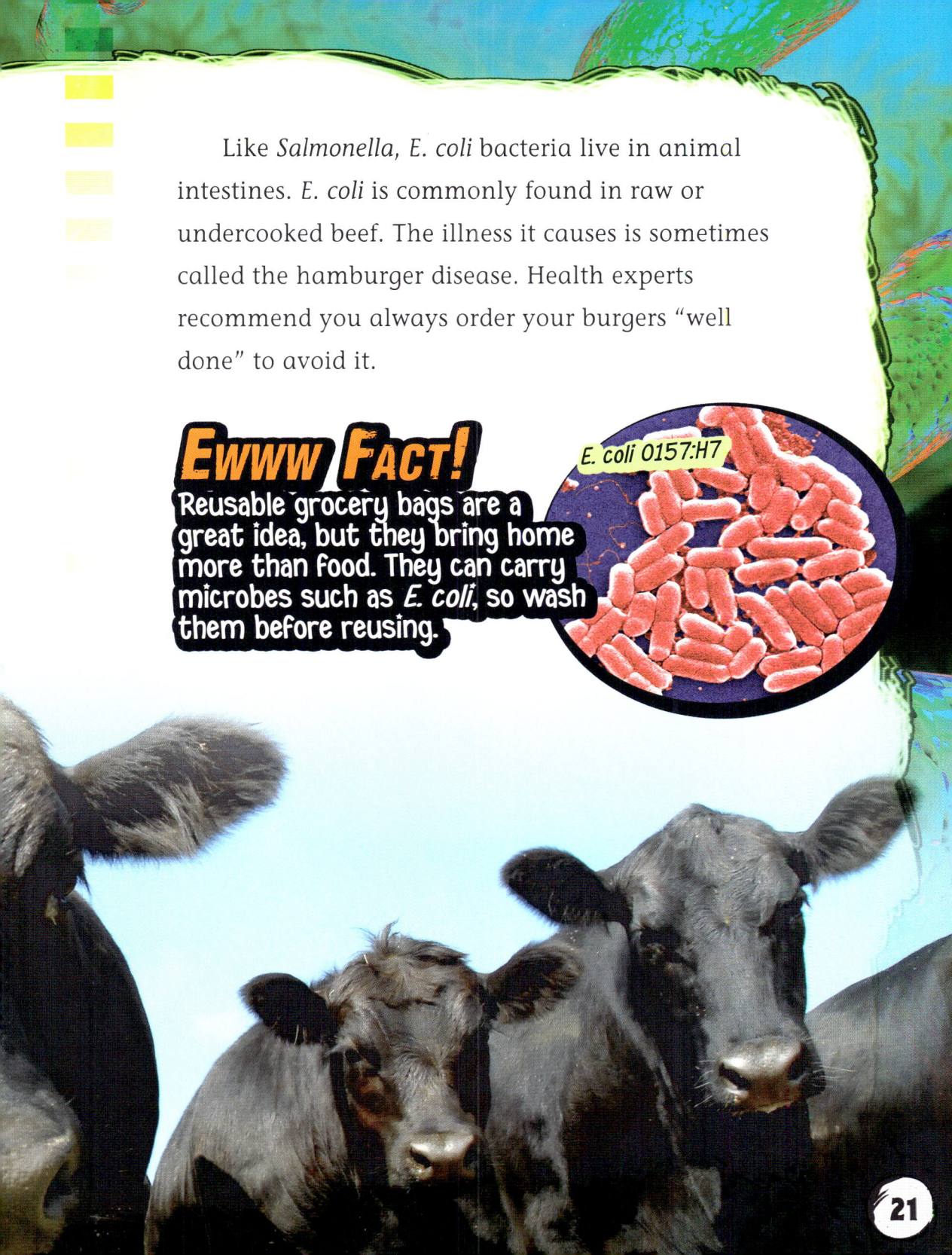

E. coli O157:H7

E. COLI OUTBREAK

One *E. coli* outbreak in Nevada, Washington, California, and Idaho was major news in 1993. Hamburger meat at a restaurant chain had *E. coli* in it, and it wasn't cooked well enough to kill the germs. More than 500 people got sick, and four people died from eating the contaminated meat.

People can spread *E. coli* too. The bacteria can live in human poop. Infected food workers can spread these dangerous germs if they don't wash their hands after using the bathroom. It's good practice for everyone to wash hands often—especially before and after handling food. You never know what dangerous microscopic creatures are lurking on your hands.

Ewww Fact!

When health officials find harmful bacteria in food, they recall it so people won't get sick. In 2010 40 food products were recalled in the United States.

Chapter 3
GOOD FOOD FRIENDS

So far all the microbes in our food sound like bad news. But we're not done yet. Bacteria can do good things too, like changing milk into yogurt, cheese, or sour cream. Microbes are so important that we add *more* microbes to milk to make these foods.

Two types of bacteria are added to pasteurized milk to make yogurt. These bacteria cause **fermentation** when they break down the lactose. Lactic acid is created. The acid makes the milk tart and thickens it into yogurt. This process is different from letting the bacteria grow naturally and spoiling the milk. Carefully adding the bacteria changes the milk's form, but doesn't spoil it.

fermentation—a chemical changing of food by microbes such as yeast and bacteria

Cheese starts with pasteurized milk too. Then helpful microbes called starter bacteria are added. These bacteria create the lactic acid. The acid breaks down the milk into solids, which are called curds, and liquid, which is called whey.

Then a substance called rennet is added to the mix. Rennet comes from the stomach of a calf or other animal. It makes the curds more solid. Soon, you have cheese.

cheese factory

MORE MILK-LOVING MICROBES

Some tasty fungi help cheeses too. The mold *Penicillium roqueforti* is added to make blue cheeses. It creates a blue color and a special flavor. Another mold, *Penicillium candidum*, grows on cheese surfaces. It gives cheeses like Camembert and Brie their flavor.

Just remember that some molds can produce dangerous mycotoxins. Don't eat moldy cheese if the mold isn't supposed to be there.

blue cheese

BREAD'S RISING

Do you like the scent of fresh-baked bread? Then you like fungus! Baker's yeast is a microscopic, single-celled fungus that makes bread dough rise. Without it, bread would be flat. Yeast makes bread dough fluffier by turning sugars into carbon dioxide gas. The carbon dioxide fills air pockets in the dough, sort of like blowing up balloons.

Ewww Fact!
Microbes help make other foods too, such as vinegar, olives, soy sauce, and pickles.

IS IT CHOCOLATE YET?

cocoa beans

The cacao tree, *Theobroma cacao*, doesn't look like a chocolate tree. The football-shaped seedpods don't look, taste, or smell like chocolate either. So when do these seeds become chocolate? After microbes do their job.

Workers pick the pods, chop them open, and spread out the seeds and pulp. Microbes show up to help the seeds ferment. The microbes come from workers' hands, tools, the air, and the soil. These microbes start the long process of changing the bitter beans into sweet chocolate. Way to go, microbes!

coprolites

Ewww Fact!
Coprolites are ancient dried poop found in waste pits. Scientists study coprolites to learn what people ate long ago and which microbes lived on their food.

THEY'RE EVERYWHERE

Microbes are everywhere, and it's a good thing because we need them. Without microbes, many of the foods we love wouldn't be around.

Of course, there are the troublemakers. Some microbes make our bread moldy and rot our fruit. Harmful germs can get into our food and cause illness. We share the world—and our kitchen—with these microbes. But there are things we can do to protect ourselves from them. Cook food well and store it safely. Eat food while it's still fresh. And wash your hands before touching your food.

So enjoy that apple. Just wash up first.

Glossary

antibiotic (an-ti-bye-OT-ik)—a drug that kills bacteria and is used to cure infections and disease

bacterium (bak-TEER-ee-uhm)—a single-celled microscopic creature that exists everywhere in nature

contaminated (kuhn-TA-muh-nay-tuhd)—unfit for use because of contact with a harmful substance

fermentation (fur-men-TAY-shun)—a chemical changing of food by microbes such as yeast and bacteria

fungus (FUHN-guhs)—a living thing that breaks down natural material; molds, mildew, yeasts, and mushrooms are fungi

microbe (MYE-krobe)—a living thing that is too small to see without a microscope

microscopic (mye-kro-SKAH-pik)—too small to be seen without a microscope

nutrient (NEW-tree-uhnt)—a substance needed by a living thing to stay healthy

outbreak (OWT-brayk)—when a number of people get sick at the same time from the same germ source

pasteurization (pas-tyur-ih-ZAY-shun)—heating process for killing harmful microbes in milk and some other liquids

Read More

Biskup, Agnieszka. *The Surprising World of Bacteria with Max Axiom, Super Scientist.* Graphic Science. Mankato, Minn.: Capstone Press, 2010.

Stille, Darlene R. *Recipe for Disaster: The Science of Foodborne Illness.* Headline Science. Mankato, Minn.: Compass Point Books, 2010.

Taylor-Butler, Christine. *Food Safety.* A True Book. New York: Children's Press, 2008.

Internet Sites

FactHound offers a safe, fun way to find Internet sites related to this book. All of the sites on FactHound have been researched by our staff.

Here's all you do:

Visit www.facthound.com

Type in this code: 9781429665322

Check out projects, games and lots more at
www.capstonekids.com

Index

antibiotics, 8

bacteria, 10, 11, 12, 16–19, 20–23, 24–25
bread, 8–10, 27, 29

cheese, 4, 8, 24–26
chicken, 18
chocolate, 4, 28
coprolites, 28
cows, 21, 25

E. coli, 20–22
eggs, 18
expiration dates, 12

fermentation, 24, 28
food poisoning, 16–23
fruits, 4, 11, 13, 14, 29
fungi, 6, 8–10, 13–15, 26, 27

ice cream, 18
illnesses, 4, 9, 10, 11, 15, 16–19, 20–22, 29
intestines, 21
Irish Potato Famine, 15

lactic acid, 12, 24–25
late blight, 15

meat, 11, 16, 18, 21–22
milk, 4, 11, 12, 24–25
mold, 6–8, 10, 13, 14, 26, 29
mycotoxins, 10, 26

outbreaks, 18, 19, 20, 22

Pasteur, Louis, 11
pasteurization, 11, 12, 24–25
penicillin, 8

recalls, 23
refrigerators, 6, 7, 11, 12
rennet, 25
reptiles, 19

Salmonella, 16–19, 21

"Typhoid Mary", 19

undercooked food, 16, 18, 21, 22

vegetables, 11, 14, 15

waste, 13, 19, 22, 28

yeast, 27
yogurt, 24